A Maze in Grace

Denise Dwyer D'Errico

Formatting RikHall.com

A Maze in Grace / Denise Dwyer D'Errico —1st ed.

ISBN-13: 978-1505366655
ISBN-10: 1505366658

Contents

Introduction 7

Fire 1
    Platform 9 ¾ 2
    Missing 4
    Mosaic 5
    Dilly Dilly 6
    Reflection 7
    Labyrinth 9
    Life 12

Water 13
    Dual Diagnoses 14
    Hyperlexia Heaven 17
    Catching Stars 19
    Remote Preparation 21
    Maps 24
    Dante 26

Earth 27
    Someone New 28
    Reflections 30
    Neighbor 32
    Phone Home 34
    Journey 35
    Time 36
    Key Change 37
    Pivot 39

Love 40
    Jenny Lin 41
    Autumn 45
    Déjà Vu 46
    Fetal Position 48
    Gut 50
    Moded 57

Detour... 60
To Forgive or Not to Forgive 62
Mermaid in Texas... 66

Thought 68
At Least 69
Let It Go.. 71
Scars & Stripes.. 73
Twist 74
Theory of Autism 75
Worrywart 78
Double-Take 80
Centering.. 82
Tsunami.. 85
Left of Center... 87

Light.. 89
Two Steps 90
Breakthrough.. 92
Key 94
Fractal 96
Clover Leaf 98
Chaos 100
After All 101
Wading.. 103
Review: Joe vs. the Volcano 105
Luck, Be a Lady.. 109
Reflection 112
Mystic 114
Midnight 115

Sound 117
Journey... 118
Miracles.. 119
Music of the Spheres.. 122
Labyrinths 124
Shiny 129
U-Turn 130
Conscious Reawakening 133
Nine 134
What I Know 136
Denouement.. 138

*I dedicate
this book
to my dear friends
and family
You are the Music
of my life*

With Gratefulness
for my
stellar angels~*
Kate, Dana, Dani, Debbie,Tracey
You Lift Me Up

Introduction

Realizing

My writing

has led me

to a journey of

self-discovery

that I didn't expect.

The Cretan labyrinth

approaches the Center

upon entrance,

but turns outward,

making three turns outside the radius.

After the third pass,

approaching the Center again,

making four more circles until,

the Center.

I started to see

my own life path

as maiden, mother, crone

in the phases and passes of the labyrinth.

The naive maiden approaches the Center,

turning from the Center and traveling outward.

She marries, bears children, sacrifices

as a mother.

Growing into a crone,

Perceiving the story

Singing the song.

After sixteen years,

I'm rediscovering my journey-

toward the Center,

as a crone,

as a mentor,

teacher,

integrator-

and my purpose.

Fire

Enter in

with intention

knowing

who you want to be

yet unchallenged

energy

Platform 9 ¾

I hide inside others' perceptions of me

Because it's easy

I let you see

what you want to see

one-dimensional me

But I am on a journey

Self-discovery

Authenticity

Breaking free

Shadows within

shadows about.

I can begin

to see the way out

Ordinary time

mythic metaphoric

call to adventure

wait for it

I don't know where I'm going.

Won't you come, too?

Missing

missing

reminiscing

my younger self

pen in hand

poetry broke forth

handwritten,

genuine

twenty years

i've only blinked

technology

advanced

or so we think

me,

i miss ink

Mosaic

tiny rocks and pretty colors juxtaposed

memories and images unfold

some of them are dazzling, others dull

altogether recreating something whole

watercolor destinies ebb and flow

mosaic synchronicity kaleidoscopes

ever changing possibility and timeless space

modulates into another sacred place

Dilly Dilly

My lavender's blue,

with crystal indigo hue,

creative helper.

Silent intuit,

feeling perceptive, Type B,

Life on island time.

All that matters is

maintain my low blood pressure,

be here for my child.

Someday I'll teach him

Enneagram theory

and, of course, Haiku.

Reflection

I can't recall exactly

how my obsession sparked

and kindled this time.

Maybe a title of a book?

Coming off one all-consuming project

looking for another

questing an obsession

led to reflection

I look in the mirror

and my arrested development

becoming apparent.

My outward appearance

not at all as I feel.

I still feel about twenty-seven.

Back then I felt nineteen

Thought I was just pretending

to be an adult

Surely someone would rat me out

But now

as I gaze upon this stranger

in the mirror

now I am

an adult

pretending to be young

Labyrinth

Enter at the front,

slight off-Center,

confidently step

towards the middle.

I can see it.

It is my destination,

my heart line.

I feel a gravitational pull,

but

my path turns left.

Turning around the circle,

I orbit the sun

until

my path bends away from

the heavenly star.

I sense it still.

Though I am further from it,

this turn is longer.

The seasons have changed.

DENISE DWYER D'ERRICO

At the end of this line,

my path turns again.

I'm fighting the current of time,

treading water.

The pass is the longest yet,

furthest from the Center.

It's but a distant light

from my cosmic outer limits.

Just when I am dreading

the next turning point,

my path takes me closer, closer

than ever before.

(Still there's more.)

A strangely familiar bend,

coming back again.

I see the Center

from the opposite direction.

Twists and turns

have changed my perspective.

I'm starting to sense

the journey is my friend.

Closer, then further,

keeping me guessing.

Like reading a story,

narrative misdirection.

One turn forward,

two turns back,

and around again.

Though further than two turns before,

not as far or as long

as my first.

Three passes,

finally the Rosette,

True North.

Dare I enter?

After so long,

I've come to the Center,

reverent peace,

calm water.

And now I understand,

my journey

begins again

in a new dimension.

Life

Unicursal life,

narrative misdirection,

Cretan labyrinth.

Water

Moon tides

cerulean waves

crashing

pushing

to create

Just wait.

The tidal wave

awakes

Dual Diagnoses

Sweet child

under three

Tested

autism

Speech therapy

begun

Concurrent

two small bumps

finger and thumb

developed

Coarse

scratchy

Doctor, consulted

whereupon—

she discouraged treatment

Over the counter meds

actually burn

young sensitive skin

and cause the warts

to grow back

We called them spots

Special

and kissed them

Then the spots

ceased

DENISE DWYER D'ERRICO

Disappeared

Erased

"Spots all gone,"

He told me

with words

Two miracles

Hyperlexia Heaven

Last week I had the pleasure of taking my sweet three-and-a-half year-old son to the library for the first time. We talked about it for days before we went on Saturday. He wanted to go all day Friday, but our local library is closed on Fridays. His anticipation was palpable and contagious. I don't know why I didn't think of it before. The local library is like Heaven for the hyperlexic child.

[Hyperlexia is described as a precocious ability to read, often beyond level of comprehension, accompanied by other social/ self-help delays. The challenge of parenting a child who is hyperlexic include providing new reading material for the insatiable little reader, as well as providing ample opportunity for review/ discussion/application in order to boost comprehension.]

So I bring my little one to the library on Saturday morning, and I give him a little tour, saying that this is the same library that Mommy used to go to when she was a little girl. Child got a kick out of this and repeated it several times, gleefully and quite loudly, whilst skipping/galloping through the main reference areas. I hurriedly steered the happy little galloper back towards the children's area. The children's librarian was not on duty, so we hopped on the MS-DOS computer terminal for the children's catalog, and did a subject search: CARS. We were delighted to discover that a familiar author had written a new picture book entitled "Sleepy Cadillac," and that it was in our library! We checked the shelf.

I engaged the little one (and he's really not little at 41 inches and 40 lbs) in assisting me locate said book. Told him to look at two shelves of H books, Mommy would look at the other two shelves of H books, and we'd race to see who could find the book entitled *Sleepy Cadillac*, first. He was very excited about this. Reading and racing and looking for books about cars. Can't get any better than that. Found the book under "new" on the next shelf, and he read aloud almost the entire book upon his immediate sitting. I had to interrupt him, saying "Save it for Later," explaining that we'd be borrowing this book to take it home and read it at home for THREE WEEKS. How exciting. Picked up three more books, including a new Tomie de Paola book, *Angels, Angels, Everywhere!*

Such a special time. He is in love with the *Sleepy Cadillac* book, reading it daily, lovingly.

Catching Stars

Every night

as I bathe the baby,

I am astounded by my good fortune.

Watching her grow and learn,

nothing short of watching a flower unfold,

every day.

I am astounded by her beauty,

and her temperament.

I think, "I'm so lucky!"

Truly, because God gave her to us.

And even though we weren't ready as soon as we hoped,

when we finally were ready,

she was there for us.

Clearly, intended for us to be her parents.

Somehow she resembles me,

and yet she is cuter than I ever was.

And who else could endure the year

of her baby's bladder problems

and subsequent surgery?

I see her reach for her Daddy,

who just melts.

I watch her older brother

already trying to teach her,

and being so helpful.

He holds her hand,

walks with her,

and encourages her to copy him,

and even entertains her,

making her giggle!

And I think,

"Wow, our family was truly meant to be."

I am humbled,

by this awesome gift we have received:

the gift of parenting.

And I am inspired to be the best mother I can be.

I feel like the luckiest girl in the world.

Because I have caught a shooting star.

Twice.

Remote Preparation

Many years ago

and just yesterday

I read a book

dense with passion

that I didn't quite get

But I understood

breakthroughs

something

preparing you

for some unknown

purpose

in time

Unlike

textbook learning

Algebra serves its purpose

X% of A equals B

One can never predict

The future revelation

How could I have known

that teaching adult

volunteer choirs to sing diphthongs

would help me teach

my autistic son

how to speak?

"Wes," he would say for Yes.

"Wellow" for yellow.

Why?

That's why.

The word *Why* starts with a W.

So I said, "Say 'E-Yes'

'E-Yellow'"

Soon his speech

flowed

like music

Just like the movie scripts

use all the parts

In Raiders of the Lost Ark

her drinking

serves a purpose

later in the story

So it is with us,

in the stories of our lives

Maps

Cross country driving

is boring.

Unless, of course,

you get to help drive.

I think it was Oklahoma City

where we got lost.

Dad was at some museum,

Mom was driving us,

She insisted she wasn't lost,

"I'm just... missing!"

Although she's speaking English

Something is lost in translation

My sister and I,

frightened,

concerned,

that we were truly lost

in the depths

of the Bible Belt.

Later Mom explained,

she had been using a skyscraper

as her mark.

Once I asked my dad,

"How many blocks from the BART station

to the theater?"

He drew me a map.

Ten block radius,

detailed street names,

even a cable car.

Now my son,

the map master,

aces geography bees,

teaches his sister

the capital of Brkina Faso

is Ouagadougo.

It's a small world,

after all.

Dante

knew

you have to

descend

to ascend

So, too,

the hero's journey

and three act form

Conflict within

begins again

Only then

can one

transcend

Earth

Shipwrecked

Sandy shores

Survival

Something more

Karma is

what you asked for

Someone New

I have always believed

when you meet someone new

who asks about you,

It is God,

checking in.

And if you should be

so lucky,

that that person says,

"Good job!"

Then you know you are

on the right path.

Life is not a straight line,

on a chart or graph.

A labyrinth,

a maze,

crazed.

Challenges,

changing mind,

ripples, detours,

wrinkles in time.

Sometimes the hard lesson

is a blessing.

Tears welling

is telling.

Washing away

part of you

and your point of view.

Reflections

What am I doing?

Why am I here?

Where am I going?

Why do I fear?

Moving on.

Where do I go now?

Where do I belong?

Surely not where I am now.

Surely not where I come from.

This is madness.

It's chaos.

I'm surrounded by idiots,

who don't even know how to read

between the lines

of reality

are poetry

and prose

and angels and miracles

and God only knows.

Every book I read,

every person I meet,

is a window,

to new possibility.

Every book I read,

every person I meet,

is a mirror,

of what's inside of me.

Inside of me.

Neighbor

As the crow flies,

It is only a mile,

But there is no road.

Fifteen minutes,

Eight lights.

It's a new day,

I'm in a new car,

With my new family,

But as I drive up the street,

I reach for my garage door opener,

As if it were still my house,

Every time.

My new home phone,

Begins the same,

I sometimes call my parents

When I mean to call home.

My husband says he does, too.

Phone Home

At church it seemed,

the ministers were phoning it in.

I suddenly knew what that meant.

My own mouth

in a silent "O,"

because I realized,

I was doing it too.

You

Are

Here.

Indeed.

Need to phone a friend.

Journey

Driving to my childhood home

my children in tow

The new Journey lead sings

strong like Young Steve Perry

Piano ostinato

sweet guitar solo

round the bend

take me away

to the eighties again

Red light.

My baby cries.

And my son says,

"Who's crying now, Mommy?

Lia, that's who!"

And I'm back.

Time

Eludes me.

Spinning galaxy.

Working nine to six.

Mapping the weekends.

Shopping lists.

Halfway through the month.

A year has blinked.

The day snails.

My kids are taller.

And brighter.

I'm older.

Wider.

Have I paid all the bills?

I just need a glass of wine.

and some more

time.

Key Change

Once upon a melody

in a minor key

depressive obsessive

darker side of me

Tidal waves and cymbals

crashed

The moment after

silence

Winds whisper

whistling

crescendo

violins and tympani

Symphonic, sonic waves

lifting me

enervate

modulate

turn the page

change the key

The lighter, brighter

centered me

Pivot

Rushing through the day,

Like it's the amazing race,

Who am I racing, anyway?

The world spins,

Making time

a game I can't win.

Two steps forward, three turns away.

Can't remember what I meant to say,

Maybe on another day.

I used to be eloquent,

I wonder where that talent went?

I wonder is she

still inside of me?

Or just someone that I used to be?

Love

Hurting, feeling

heart is bleeding

Learning

The world is turning

Giving and forgiving

living and forgetting

Loving

Remembering

Jenny Lin

Young girl,

middle-school musician,

dancer, soccer player,

destined for greatness.

Horrific random rape and murder,

in the bath of her own home.

Her parents,

in anguish

but searching for hope

in something so devastating,

create a memorial concert

in her name.

Twenty years later,

I raise my own family

in the neighborhood

on the hill.

We attend the memorial concert,

band, symphony, and choir,

amazingly talented students,

but they do not know her.

Her parents, the foundation,

honored by the nation's government.

A congressional certificate,

praising their work.

Mistress of ceremony,

local news celebrity.

The love and support

from the congregation,

is music in itself.

Energy,

rises and falls.

Silence and applause.

Wondrous opportunity

for the students.

With heavy heart,

I watch and listen

with my children.

Do they understand?

I cannot tell them

how she died.

I do not want them to be scared.

My daughter so young.

My son so innocent.

Like the young girl,

her picture on the program,

Twenty years ago

and just yesterday.

This summer music program,

A bench at middle school,

A room at the library,

The annual candlelight vigil,

all in her memory.

Her parents have been through

hell and back,

and they have made music

in her name.

But it's not the same.

I know

they'd give anything

to have her back

again.

Autumn

Leaves fall

winds sing

Descending

Last year

I was here

Depressing

Heavy

Reverie

Telling

Déjà Vu

The world has turned

another year

I'm still here

struggling

dieting

wondering

denying

Treading water

is all I can do

Somehow, I matter less

I get one wish

a mani-pedi

But I can't relax

planning spaghetti

for the family

even though I'm gluten free.

If I can just get through

this month

But I haven't the strength

to single-handedly

plan a family vacation.

Too busy to change

the calendar page

Time

crashes

like waves

Splashes

and I age

Fetal Position

Invisible bags of heavy, wet sand,

press down on me,

I can't breathe.

Feeling like I'm a total failure

In life, work,

living, and parenting.

One thought

corkscrews and loops

I can't unthink it

Nobody cares

People don't understand

I seethe

in slowly,

suffering in

self-criticism.

Collapsing,

falling in,

descending,

again.

I crawl in bed,

my blanket,

my only friend.

Gut

Lower right

abdominal

tightening

Like an invisible fis,

crushing my insides

I'm certain my organs

have shredded

sharp and constant

If I could just vomit

I might feel

better

Breathe through

yogic mudra gestures

desperate attempt

pulling at threads

I've sunken into

the quicksand

of despair

every month

like clockwork

First I thought it was the flu

then acid reflux

driving to Walmart

on a quick break

desperately seeking

some platitude pill

On the way to the hospital

I found relief

in placebo

and a prayer

Parked on the rooftop

napped in the sun

sonogram upon my wake

Maybe it's dairy

He said

Quit milk

Maybe it's caffeine

He said

Quit that

Apple cider vinegar shot of pectin

in apple juice

tonic of choice

Sonogram

showed

freaking gallbladder is

killing me

No amount of pectin

can help me now

Did I do this to myself?

Feels worse than birth.

That was easy

compared to this.

Plus then, I got a beautiful baby.

But now

I get

burned

from the inside out.

Breathe the

burden of responsibility

when the boss calls me in

and I pretend

that I don't have to bend

that I can stand straight, tall

and walk.

I'm the only employed parent

I can't lose my job

and so I continue

following the stupid diet

No fat

No fun

No fair

Until one day

on vacation

involuntarily

I purge

DENISE DWYER D'ERRICO

the pizza

pepperoni

bile, green

vile, mea.

This isn't normal.

Booked the surger.

Take that, gall bladder!

I don't need YOU anymore.

HA!

Drinking the sleepy juic,

like Hawaiian Punch

in a Dixie paper cu,

My husband saying

I was so luck,

"Gonna have the best nap ever,"

in that singsong way

we talk to our children.

My surgeon, typically so

impeccably well-dressed,

sitting at a laptop computer

wild, wild hair,

like he had just had

His best nap ever.

Mad Scientist Trope.

My last fleeting thought

When I awoke,

they showed me

gall stones.

Dried, petrified peas,

pearled and wrinkled,

some the size of raisins.

Scars

on my stomach

small, really

but the post-surgery,

the bag of air

pressuring my back.

No wonder

people think they are having

a heart attack.

DENISE DWYER D'ERRICO

After sitting on the couch all day,

I brush my teeth,

and fall asleep

in the same place.

Could it be?

All this crap happened,

So I could take some time for myself?

Moded

Childhood taunt.

To me, it sounded like molded.

but I guess it was moded all along.

I thought it was molded.

"You thought it was mole dead!"

"Nanny, nanny, billy goat!"

"MO dead!"

"Whatever do you mean?"

Pretending it didn't hurt.

I have seen

my son's eyes

when his friends

would take his hat

in keep away.

He was smiling

through his frustration.

He said, "They were playing with me."

"Sometimes it's hard for me to find someone to play

with."

I am eight years old,

again.

Befriending

two best friends

who turned on me.

They called me

and told me

they can't be friends with me

anymore.

Goodbye.

Click.

Piercing dial tone,

knifed my heart.

Avocado crescent

In its cradle

And I cried

My son does not cry

But I,

with my moded,

broken heart,

know.

Detour

Something about a u-turn

Challenges.

Clover leaf,

Spinning,

Circles.

You never go anywhere.

Detours,

Are signed,

Well-lined.

Still get there,

Later.

Much, much later.

Battered and worn,

From time and space.

But was it all

A waste?

Taking the time,

To stop,

And smell the coffee,

I mean, roses.

See?

Annoying as those detours were,

We are better for them.

To Forgive or Not to Forgive

They asked for my forgiveness.

I didn't want to

At first

I didn't really know how

I couldn't let it go

I mean,

I was right, after all,

And they were wrong.

Castle Walls

Were not coming down.

But in time

I decided

I wanted to show to my children

That I was the type of person

Who could forgive

So I decided

Swallow my pride

Look them in the eye

And tell them

I Forgive You

I was not prepared for

the peace it would bring me

immediately

invisible chains

had been holding me

and now I was free

Our friendship

Returned to Happy.

Then I asked someone else

For her forgiveness,

Denied.

A door had closed on her heart

Slamming on our friendship

And I realized

Forgiveness wasn't coming,

Like, ever

because she wasn't ready for it.

And I've been there.

The lack of love

Had transformed me

into an ugly beast

And I longed to counsel her

Judgment, grief,

Hope, belief

but I knew that would be

barking up the wrong tree

somehow, making it worse.

Still I struggled

I couldn't let it go

I was right, you know

Miracle in my Twitter feed

A link to an article to read

Forgiveness

may not mean reconciliation

It may mean

separation

Choirs sing

Realizing

Freedom is coming.

I realized I needed to forgive her

For her inability

To forgive me

I had apologized

and made several attempts at reconciliation

my former friend has not forgiven me

but God has.

Forty years running

with the catholic church

and I only just learned

forgiveness

Mermaid in Texas

Charmed by the cowboy

Wed in human form

True Love Forever

Birthed two strapping young ones

But the cursed blood red moon

Tides pulled her love away

To the trenches of the ocean

Ne'er to be seen again

Serena in sorrow

Cried to tears of stars

Howled to the moon

Why, o why?

Boys grow

Next thing she knows

Another cowboy, her friend

Invites her in

This mermaid

Has learned

She can love

Again

It's not

That she's forgot

Her children's father

How could she

She's remembered

Herself

Integrated the grief

And the sorrow

Into a new tomorrow

Perceiving possibility

achieve believability

knowing there is so much more

Some things are worth striving for

At Least

Chatting with a co-worker

About our kids

My son with his autism

a-typical development

reading before speaking

walking database

with few friends

His girls have allergies

EPI-pens

Everywhere

They can't even go

to Five Guys

Peanuts everywhere,

anaphylactic shock

He says to me:

"At least it isn't Autism!"

And I am thinking,

At least Autism is not fatal!

Let It Go

In my favorite café

I want to dig i,

but the coffee grinder

obscures the cool music

It's like, what music?

Killing my vibe

Sometimes things don't work out

the way you planned

And yet

somehow, it's better

Who knew?

Letting a Zhu Zhu pet loose

in a café

Could be so much fun?

Delightful squeals

from my little one

Maybe I won't write today

maybe I'll just play

Scars & Stripes

once prominent

blood-soaked

bandaged

caked

scabbed

two short years later

faded

into stretch marks

who would have known

stretch marks

are good for something

masking

scars

Twist

Expect the unexpected.

A web article caught my eye:

Accept those inevitable exceptions.

I sat down to read it,

thinking it would be about

expecting the unexpected.

Alas,

it was about commonly confused words.

Not at all what I had expected.

Huh.

Theory of Autism

Presence

of minds

present

Presents

Social systems

Executive function

Organized thoughts

Brushing,

Is it not stimming?

Practical generalization application

Theory in real life

Life experience

Mind experience

Can we mind meld?

Systemically?

Gears turn,

Evenly unevenly,

Odds, even,

Even odds,

Odd numbers of gears,

Spin in turn,

In the same direction,

Even numbers of gears,

Turn opposite directions,

Or is it the opposite?

Maybe the square peg,

Is in tune,

And everybody else is flat.

Round holes,

Black holes,

Gateways,

New dimensions,

In Theory

of mind,

Absolutely,

Absolution.

Maybe the different ones,

Are normal,

And everybody else

is whacked.

Worrywart

I worry a lot.

I worry about a lot of things.

I try to not worry so much.

But I can't seem to stop worrying.

Lately, I've been worried about my own furrowed brow.

That's right.

I'm worrying about worrying.

So I furrow my brow even more.

Which of course worries me.

And then I can't get my face unstuck.

You see my predicament.

I tried mentally relaxing every muscle in my body, starting in my toes.

Another weird paradox in itself:

I must concentrate to do this and thus wrinkle my brow.

I get distracted before I get to my head.

So I tried starting from my scalp.

Even though I am aware of my furrowed brow,

I can't seem to relax it.

It just wants to be in its new home position.

It's like I can't remember what it feels like to not have a tensed up brow.

So I looked to Google for help.

I followed a link to Calm Your Face, Calm Your Mind.

Sounds good right?

It was a really good article.

But it was the part about the golf tees

    taped to people's eyebrows

        that did the trick

            My tension just melted into

            a laugh-out-loud smile.

            So now whenever I start to worry

            about my worry,

            or my face getting stuck-

            I just think of that article,

            and it makes me laugh again.

Double-Take

Someone took a picture

of me

and shared it

on the Internet

I thought I looked cute.

But in that photo,

I looked oh, so fat

in my new favorite dress, too

calypso blue,

like the fruit of the loom.

I un-tagged myself

(Though family photo treasures

are kept forever

like my grandfather's "No Name Club.")

But the damage was done.

And here I thought I had been doing so well.

So, so far to go.

The best that I can do

from this melancholy soup

is to remember

to call it

BEFORE.

Someday soon,

post-bathing suit,

AFTER

Looking forward to the ever after.

Centering

Listening

to my heart's wishes

the possibilities

within

dormant dreams

Awakening

to my true self

again.

I was here before,

years ago

I knew the simple joys

playing with creation

exploration

art.

Then,

marriage,

and motherhood,

turning

away from the Center.

Treading water,

as the current pulled me,

from the artist,

to the helper.

I earn a living helping others,

but I could not help

my Self.

On the edge

of my labyrinth,

after sixteen years

as a helper,

I am ready to

Turn.

Brave toward the sun,

Risk and reward are one.

Modulation,

integration

developing

harmony

The whole

as the sum of its parts,

and then some.

I am a Peacemaker,

and it is time

to resume my life path

direction toward my Soul,

leading others along the way.

Maiden inside.

Mother in stride.

Mentor, the crone

that I am

becoming.

Tsunami

In the coffee shop

by the window

Sultry jazz singer sings

Hauntingly familiar

Is it Sheryl Crow?

Too subtle for

my music reading app

to detect

over the din

of grinding

coffee beans.

But then,

a familiar face

swims to memory's surface.

It is Fiona Apple

from her first album,

I didn't get her then.

Maybe I should listen to

the tidal wave

again?

Maybe this time

understanding

will be

like a tsunami,

carrying me away

to another place,

and time.

Funny how music

becomes the soundtrack

of our lives,

and the score,

heard before,

only foreshadows

something more.

Left of Center

Reconsidering.

Reflection.

Misdirection.

It seems A

does lead

to B.

Albeit

circuitously.

Longing for the Center,

only to be

redirected,

annoyingly.

The sparkly thing

that beckons me

from my path perceived.

Such conceit.

As if,

a girl can dream.

Synchronicity.

Where I need to be.

Weaving, winding,

discerning, deciding.

Decisions.

Decisions.

Payday!

A ha, a ha!

As if life were a board game.

I only know,

that I don't always know.

And that's okay.

Save it for another day.

My labyrinthine

wandering

Is the way.

Light

bursts forth

and angels sing

intuition awakening

feel the rhythm

speak the rhyme

chaos dissolves

into sacred time

Two Steps

forward,

I can see the Center.

But I am turning

left,

and left again.

Backwards.

Two steps forward,

one step back.

Grapevine.

Step behind,

Step touch.

Bounce.

Skip.

What am I doing?

I'm just dancing,

Away

from the Center.

I don't care.

I'll get there.

Someday.

Maybe, today

I just dance.

Breakthrough

An hour or ten.

I've done it again.

Musing, writing,

Theorizing.

Plan to have fun.

The caffeine hasn't hit me yet.

But I must admit,

The week I didn't eat

Gluten or grains-

My eczema, constipation, and fear

Disappeared.

I don't even remember

having forgotten them.

One day,

Ghosts and demons

have gone away.

Many signs perceived,

Message received.

Indirection

Is the direction.

Perfect imperfection.

Indecision

Is the

Musing

my mission?

Key

Spinning the Greek key,

makes a labyrinth.

Read, perceive,

signs of dys-health.

Developing Sonata

Circling the theme

Dances

ever so slightly,

on the edge.

But the gravitational pull

to recapitulation,

and the theme is reached again

I am home.

The end

is the completion

of the song.

And it is time

To begin

a new movement.

Fractal

As I sit and write

I can't help but notic,

all these good-looking men

Likely salesmen

chiselled, bespectacled

crisp, cuff links

My husband

frequents these cafés, too

Women probably

notice him

no doubt

Somewhere,

some other woman

could be noticing

My husband

Right now

Maybe she

is even writing

about him

Similar scenes

devices and screens

Parallel lives

Stories happening

Clover Leaf

Hungry,

longing for,

filet mignon.

Feeling guilty,

thinking of,

the long lunch.

Exited early,

tried to get back on,

the highway.

In the same direction,

alas a clover leaf,

delivered me.

Towards the East,

cursing, sighing, navigating,

back to the Highway.

Westward bound, Hell,

I don't even like this restaurant

anymore.

I like the other one better.

Inspired, called ahead for takeout.

drove to the further place.

Curbside delivery,

back in under

an hour.

At my desk,

sweet desk,

executive wing.

They are all out today.

I can feast

in peace.

Chaos

Fractal philosophy

Relative derivative

Chaotic patterns

Broccoli and genealogy

The Greek key is labyrinthine

Mosaic mandala

Kaleidoscope universe

Chairos

After All

When I find myself

lost,

misled,

questing a quest,

create my turn,

with my own purple crayon,

write out

of the rut.

Knowing,

the quest for the Center,

is the path.

And almost as soon as you reach the Center,

it's time,

to turn around,

and go back.

As soon as you think,

you are enlightened,

you most certainly,

are not.

We are not monks.

We are not addicts.

We must return

to this life,

and forge

the seemingly serpentine

circuitous path.

Logarithms,

loop,

and progress.

New levels,

new quests.

It is our destiny,

to quest.

How else

can I priestess,

but having gone through

this mess?

Wading

Rolling with the punches,

Rolling in the Deep

wade in the water

God's a-gonna trouble the water

Moontides.

Wading the beach,

sand beneath my feet.

It's not easy, it is sand after all.

Sometimes it's quicksand,

and I wipe out.

Just need

to breathe

and decide

to ride

the waves

Peaceful rocking

there is movement

and energy

in being still

finally

I don't know

where the waves will take me

what the water brings me

Pretty shells and treasures

or broken glass

Review: Joe vs. the Volcano

When I was in college there was a movie that came out starring Tom Hanks and Meg Ryan. No, not the one you think it is. The other one. No not that one, either. Are you ready? It was called <u>Joe vs. the Volcano</u>. I enjoyed it immensely. I have not found anyone else who likes it as much as I do. In fact, the world didn't like it. The industry forgot about it. And I am the only one, it seems, who remembers the story.

It's a mythic satire. Really, any movie with a title of <u>Joe vs. the Volcano</u> should give you a little bit of a clue. This is not realism, and it is not even realistic fiction. Basically, the Tom Hanks character works in a life-draining desk job. We don't know what he does exactly, but it doesn't matter. Meg Ryan is his co-worker in her first of three quirky characters. Honestly, now that I am a working adult, I can appreciate this part of the story so much more. The fluorescent lights in the windowless dungeon of an office seem to suck the life out of your eyeballs, says Hanks. Meg cannot even function. Been there.

The company logo and a theme of the film is this twisted jagged lightning bolt. The path to the work office. The lava flowing from the volcano (later) flows in this pattern. Have you ever seen a symbol recur seemingly everywhere?

I have to watch this movie again. I rented it twelve years ago and no one would watch it with me. I bet I could get it used, for cheap. Somehow, Hanks is diagnosed with a fatal brain cloud. He meets Ryan in her second incarnation, the redheaded artist. They are each lost in their own worlds. Ryan's art is desperate, meta, and dramatic. She recites a poem that to this day, I still recall:

Long ago,

The delicate tangles of his hair,

Covered,

The emptiness of my hand.

Would you like to hear it again? She says. He says yes, but she begins the dramatic retelling again and he stops her.

Somehow the artist must deliver him to her sister, also played by Meg Ryan. Here is where we see Ryan as we recognize Ryan, blonde and perky, finally. The sisters discuss how they haven't seen their father, the elusive millionaire who needs Hanks to jump into a volcano. Yes, this is weird. Just go with it. Suspend that disbelief. You can do it.

They are shipwrecked and have only Hanks' four wardrobes. He strings them together as a raft, the unconscious Ryan splayed across them. Somehow he manages to change her outfits whilst she is unconscious. Like a Barbie doll, she is seen outfitted for several scenes of play. Hanks plays golf on his floating island, soon they are out of drinking water and he gives rations to the comatose one. Castaway plus one.

So they arrive at the island, a wild pseudo-Polynesian pre-civilization which has maddeningly discovered Orange Soda. How hilarious is this? Remember *The Gods Must Be Crazy*? The couple is separated for preparation for the feast (in which Joe will jump into the erupting volcano to assuage the gods). The females of the island pamper Meg with creams and massage. A Vanuatuan spa. In contrast, Hanks is pounded by the island males. Pounded. This is played for humorous effect.

The couple marches up the mountain to the volcano's mouth. Joe believes he is dying anyway so he is ready to jump. Ryan suddenly announces her feelings for him. And so the tribal king marries them. And they jump together. But it is a leap of faith. And the wafts of the volcano blow them to the open sea, where they find their trusty luggage, miraculously. Amen! Ryan asks what was his diagnosis anyway. Joe says a brain cloud. She says this is not a thing. Turns out her daddy bought the diagnosing doctor in order to get Joe to jump into the volcano.

I love this story because the misadventure and the continuity of signs. The symbol is a crooked path. This I get. Hasn't your life been a crooked path?

One night as I was driving home from work, I noted the fresh rain glistening in the pre-sunset over the hills. And the freeway made a winding movement through the hills. It was the symbol of Joe vs. the Volcano. And I laughed like I hadn't in ages.

The way home is a crooked path.

And so it is.

Luck, Be a Lady

Weird stuff happens to me.

Just ten days ago my car died on the freeway.

I've also run out of gas

and run over a mattress.

But I also believe that I'm lucky.

I have faith and I am positive.

I have led a charmed life in many ways.

Sure, I've had my own trials and tribulations,

challenges and curve balls.

Anyone who's gone through labor knows,

you don't always get the labor you ordered.

You sure don't get the parenting experience you or-

dered.

Who requests to birth a child with special needs

or with recurring bladder infections throughout the first

year of life?

But would I have had it any other way?

What do you think?

DENISE DWYER D'ERRICO

Once had a lucky streak.

I was winning every raffle,

every table prize.

I knew the yellow ribbon was tied under my chair.

And so it was.

Some of the things I won were

the *Titanic* movie spe-cial edition on VHS

(it was 1998, okay?)

and the trip to Lake Tahoe

given by my hubby's company

every summer picnic.

I won three years in a row.

Playing Bingo.

It's not like there was any strategy.

And then one summer,

I had doubt.

I wondered if I was losing "it."

I wondered if it was someone else's turn

to be the lucky one.

I traded bingo cards with the kid next to me.

Sure enough, the eight year-old girl won the trip.

On my card!

And so I knew it was over.

Or so I perceived.

I now believe that I am lucky, again.

Or rather, I again believe that I am lucky.

Back to my dead car on the freeway,

although I did immediately understand

that we were in a precarious situation,

I never for a minute believed

we were in absolute danger.

I knew I had called for help and prayed.

I knew God was sending angels.

Luck is on my side.

Reflection

It seems I

identify

with being

unidentifiable.

I like being out of the box.

But I miss out on

having friends.

I do think

Some of my friends

wear that hat

a little too tight.

No Disney. No Apple. No trends.

No invaders. No dragons. No trolls.

Lions and tigers and bears.

As if!

And I realize

I perceive a flaw

in them,

when the flaw

is really

Within.

So caught up

in being

out of the box,

I was trapped.

Glass ceilings crack,

boundaries collapse.

Perception

enters

another

dimension.

Mystic

What is cooking but brewing?

Are not recipes but potions?

Is not homeopathy wizardry?

Jesus knew the secret.

His laying of hands was Reiki.

And the spit of clay was a spell.

The hero's journey is alchemy.

And communion is presence.

Because ritual is real.

Literal is mystic.

Midnight

On the eve

of a deadline

on the verge of a breakthrough

I feared I'd been lost

but I found

the path

Perhaps

I was meant to discover

among the dysfunction

a call to adventure

write this damn book

grapple with

structure and theme

Look! I wrote a book!

it's a meme.

Shackles of perception

broken free

Though I knew I could do it,

I thought I knew the theme,

I thought I was writing the book,

but it was writing me.

Sound

Music and poetry

making sense of reality

Centering

finally

free

Journey

a story is a circle

ring composition

foreshadowing

red herrings

remote preparation

red flags

transition

transformation

modulation

segue

turn the page

Miracles

Each year at Holy Week I reread a favorite novel: The delightful *Miracles of Santo Fico* by D.L. Smith. I remember the first time I read it ten years ago. I reveled in the story and the storytelling. Even then.

The story opens with a confession in a hot church in the forgotten little town and parish of Santo Fico. The priest contemplates his own secret sin even as he listens to the regularly occurring weekly confessions of his parishioners. I wonder what his sin could be? The characters enjoy the surprise visitation by a lost tour bus. The characters' perceptions of themselves, followed by the town folks' perceptions of them, and this change in perspective tells the whole story.

I've since amassed a kind of virtual book club of friends and family who join me in rereading this book each year. I tell them it's a story of heartbreak and humor within this sweet, forgotten Italian town. Like *Chocolat* but in Italy.

But I reread it now for different reasons. Each year at Holy Week I am in a different season of my life.

119

One year my sweet parents travelled in Italy for Holy Week. As it happened, there was a massive earthquake in one region of the country. I didn't hear from my parents for three days. I did fret some. At first. Then I became irritated with them for not calling. In truth, they were on a tour bus and weren't watching the news, as they were in a foreign country and therefore the news was not broadcast in their language. They didn't even know there had been an earthquake. They explained when they called on the third day.

I remember the Holy Week I was in darkness waiting to hear from my beloved parents. The apostles as lived in fear after the brutal killing of their prophet Jesus. The flawed characters of Santo Fico as they trudged on their perceived dreary lives in obscurity until the day the tour bus came, and Leo Pizzola gave the tourists his charming tour of the miracle and the mystery. I felt a connection, camaraderie, with them.

As I reread this story some years, and I rejoice in the laugh out loud moments as the bumbling townsfolk attempt to create their own miracles and work out their own kinks. How the fabricated miracles go wrong, not at all according to plan, and yet the truth is their mishaps reveal even greater miracles of Truth.

Now, as a writer, I reread this story reveling in the techniques. The turn of perspective, subtle delicate and poignant. Showing rather than telling. The building of anticipation towards each event. The weaving together of all moving parts the characters redemptions. The unraveling and the denouement. All in the craft of the storyteller.

What a gift. We have been given the opportunity to life and learn and reflect. We are characters in God's storybook. We fabricate our own miracles and some fizzle. We move some puzzle pieces around to where they fit.

Maybe I am playing a part in somebody else's miracle story.

Music of the Spheres

Sacraments

Labyrinths

Chakras

Saga

Journey

Rising

Descending

Neverending

Chakras

Kabbalah

Catholic symmetry

Enneagram

I know

Who I am

Love's fool

Shakespearean school

Philosophy

Theology

Alchemy

Higher key

Psychology

Mythology

Epic

Operatic story

Dante's journey below

through to Purgatorio.

You

are

here

Shh

Listen

to the music

of the spheres

Labyrinths

The moment my dear daughter awakes, she begins excitedly chattering about our day in San Francisco. In her kindergarten naïveté, she'd imagined we'd take the Golden Gate Bridge. My dear son, the geography expert, patiently listens as I explain to her that we need to take the Bay Bridge from our home. We all admire the shiny new bridge. The moment we exit on Fremont Street she squeals with delight as if we are on a roller coaster.

We are heading to Grace Cathedral, as I had read about the current artist in residence and the liturgical art experience. Twenty miles of thin ribbons hang from the cathedral ceiling. The ribbons represent both our prayers and God's love. I knew I wanted to see it and I thought my children would appreciate it, too. My in-laws were in town so they decided to join us, and they brought along their friends. So it became a motley pilgrimage. Ah, well, such is the journey.

Quite simply, the experience is majestic. The ribbons bring the light and colors from the stained glass windows into the sanctuary and across the pews. The natural light through the windows enhances the ribbons' colors.

As the clouds and winds change, the ribbons seem to move and dance in their stillness. I learned later that some of the ribbons had the actual prayers of the community written upon them. From every angle there is beauty and life. I bring my extended family to the Center of the worship space and chose a pew. My children and I kneel on the soft blue cushions conveniently stowed. "They look like suitcases!" My daughter exclaims. Once kneeling, we look up into this vast rain of color. There is no doubt that this is a sacred space. Grace is alive and present.

From here we walk the labyrinth. There are two at Grace, and we chose the one located inside the cathedral. The labyrinth is a prayerful experience in itself, as one walks toward the Center. One is to notice and acknowledge thoughts, moving away from the distractions. When one reaches the Center, one waits in silent prayer, Centering. Exiting via the same path, acknowledging the return to self, hopefully somewhat more enlightened.

I invite my son to walk himself, as I invite my daughter to hold my hand. She leads me. I want to enjoy this experience but my mind is spinning with troublesome thoughts: *I don't think she's going to hold my hand the whole time. Is my son doing it right? I wish there weren't so many people here, it's so crowded and we are all going too fast.* I'm whispering to my children to be quiet and giving them stares and telling them to keep their hands to themselves. I'm wishing that we could have a different experience. But this is my experience.

The path is narrow and winding and I think we are reaching the Center but then the path guides us away, back to the edge. I realize this is the metaphor. There aren't four paths to the Center, there's one and we will walk each quadrant. We keep bumping elbows and hips and bags and purses. My son can't help but try to push my daughter off course and tickle her. I'm frustrated because I'm trying to have a prayerful experience but they're goofing around. I keep running into my mother-in-law. I learn to reposition my cross-body purse so that it rests behind me. Now that I am walking with my purse bouncing on my big behind, I get it. Sometimes a symbol just has to jump up and spank you: no baggage on the labyrinth! I'm free with both hands now. My son has moved to lead us somehow, I hiss at him to slow down and he falls behind us now in protest. I find myself harshly whisper-explaining as I seem to do often, and I realize I don't like the sound of myself right now. So I stop. Let everyone be. We enter the Center finally, and we each choose a leaf-like alcove to pause for reflection.

My own reflection is spared in the interest of time and helping others. Typical. I'm whispering to my young daughter an improvised prayer, which she will voice for us both. I turn to my son and ask him if he prayed. He says yes. I notice my in-laws have now arrived at the Center so now we can remove ourselves from the reflection pods and begin the reverse course. I say to my son, "Show us the way." We follow him out. We meet and cross the friends, as they began later than we did. We have to maneuver a little dance to let them through as we exit. The whole thing seems to take longer than it should, and yet not long enough. I'm somewhat frustrated again, but this is how it is.

We exit the labyrinth at a baptismal font of holy water and bless ourselves. We admire some tapestry and I snap a few photos on my phone. I note that my kids are restless, and so we pick up a few pamphlets and say goodbye to our group, heading for the gift store. The friends of my in-laws say to me that they have lived just five minutes away for years and years, and yet they've never come here before. They thank me. They are really very sweet. She actually invites us to come to their house next time we come to the city.

Dear daughter wants to buy everything in the gift store, for everybody that she loves. She wants matching t-shirts for her and her brother. Finally I say she can have one book. She chooses a board book entitled, *Where is God?* and is already reading it aloud all by herself. She is delighted by the verse, "God is in the first tomato?" My heart melts in her sweetness. Dear son wants a bookmark, as he is a reader. I am drawn to an expensive book of daily Centering prayers. I guess I need Centering. I buy all of these,

127

plus a magnet featuring a sea otter for my husband, who has to work on this school holiday.

We cross the street to the parking garage. Dear daughter is enraptured by the hills so we walk a few feet down a particularly steep sidewalk for fun. Fortunately, there are steps for the way back up. Once in our car, I let the disembodied voice of the smartphone guide me down California Street towards our next destination. It's a gloriously sunny day with clear blue skies and wondrous views. I wish I could stop and take photos as we head east. As if I could. These moments are graced with wonder, as they fleetingly pass by. But life keeps going on, and more moments occur. Hills of ups and downs and one-way streets. We are not taking the most direct route to Pier 39. And why would you? When there's California Street, cable cars, and the Embarcadero. At the edge of the city we turn north, following the circle. Just like in the labyrinth. And I find myself Centered, finally. This is what it's all about. After a wonderful lunch and visit on the pier (including the funny hat store, where you must try on crazy hats and take pictures), we followed yet another route toward the Bay Bridge. Exiting the labyrinth of the city from the same entrance point, the new bridge takes us home, to our ordinary lives, to our selves.

Shiny

I should be

working on

my work in progress.

But I keep thinking about

the other books

inside [of] me.

Characters,

Stories,

Bursting

To break forth,

Into song.

If this writer

Only had the time.

U-Turn

Naïvely approaching the Center,

Not knowing,

I would be u-turned

In this amazing race.

I was an Artist,

Retreating,

Turning away from God,

Into a Helper,

As mothers do.

Finally,

Circles spin,

Beginning toward the middle again.

Approaching the Center,

Centering.

Recognizing the crone

Within.

Pursuing the Truth,

Collaging my youth,

With the teacher.

As I become

The mentor,

Friend,

Spiritual guide,

Peaceful healing empathy,

that Peacemakers know

to be true.

Conscious Reawakening

Reality and our perceptions,

that's to realize.

What is real?

What is really real?

It goes back to

what we don't know.

Knowing,

that we don't know

is enough.

Nine

What does it mean

to be a peacemaker

an empath healer

an integrator?

Body, mind, and spirit,

head, heart, and gut,

three-act theory,

pieces of the puzzle.

Embrace the pain,

Feel the angst,

Grow with it,

Let go of it.

Breathe in,

Breathe out.

The many different parts of me,

even the parts you cannot see,

all integrate

into something greater

than the sum of all parts.

The fusion

is alchemy.

And I am here

to teach.

Others guide,

to look inside.

Sing with me

your heavenly song:

Glory!

In the highest!

What I Know

I know what I know

I know what I don't know

Or rather, I don't know what I don't know

How could I know?

Why I write

is to make sense of world

Characters whisper to me

in the middle of night

Stories

plots

themes

created from my own life journey

suddenly teach me

writing is my story

I want to teach others

let them know

they are not alone.

I want my children to learn

They can write, too.

Denouement

Sometimes you gotta go left

in order to go right

Sometimes you gotta go through the dark night

in order to see the light

Sometimes you have to descend

in order to begin again

The path you take

The choices you make

Change can be a friend

Thank you for reading!

Dear Reader,

I hope you enjoyed *A Maze in Grace*. I wrote this book for you, so that you would think about your own stories, too. What's your story? I know my own story is still developing. I also have more stories to tell, including the story which I believe I was meant to write. Stay tuned for news about *The Other Side of the Ocean*.

As an author, I love feedback. You are the reason I am writing. So, tell me what you liked, what you loved, and even what you hated. I would love to hear from you.

You can write me at derricodenise@gmail.com or visit my website at www.denisederrico.wordpress.com.

Finally, I need to ask a favor. If you are so inclined, I'd love a review of *A Maze in Grace*. Loved it, hated it— I'd just enjoy the feedback. Reviews can be tough to come by these days. You, the reader, have the power to make or break a book. I invite you to take a moment to leave a review on amazon.com.

Thank you so much for reading *A Maze in Grace* and spending time with me.

Peace,

17995800R00085

Made in the USA
San Bernardino, CA
23 December 2014